MONSTROUS MANNERS

MANNERS AT THE STORE

BY BRIDGET HEOS  ILLUSTRATED BY KATYA LONGHI

Amicus Illustrated is published by Amicus
P.O. Box 1329, Mankato, MN 56002
www.amicuspublishing.us

Library of Congress Cataloging-in-Publication Data
Heos, Bridget, author.
 Manners at the store / by Bridget Heos;
illustrated by Katya Longhi.
    pages cm. – (Monstrous manners)
 "Amicus Illustrated is published by Amicus."
 Summary: "A young monster with no manners
goes grocery shopping with his dad and older
brother, who teaches him how to have manners at
the supermarket"– Provided by publisher.
 Audience: K to grade 3.
 ISBN 978-1-60753-746-5 (library binding) –
ISBN 978-1-60753-901-8 (ebook)
1. Etiquette for children and teenagers. 2. Courtesy–
Juvenile literature. 3. Stores, Retail–Juvenile
literature. I. Longhi, Katya, illustrator. II. Title.
 BJ1857.C5H464 2016
 395–dc23
                                        2014041497

Editor: Rebecca Glaser
Designer: Kathleen Petelinsek

Printed in the United States of America at
Corporate Graphics in North Mankato, Minnesota.

10 9 8 7 6 5 4 3 2 1

ABOUT THE AUTHOR

Bridget Heos is the author of more than
70 books for children, including *Mustache
Baby* and *Mustache Baby Meets His Match*.
Her favorite manners are holding the door
for others and jumping up to help. You can
find out more about her, if you please, at
www.authorbridgetheos.com.

ABOUT THE ILLUSTRATOR

Katya Longhi was born in southern Italy.
She studied illustration at the Nemo
NT Academy of Digital Arts in Florence.
She loves to create dream worlds with
horses, flying dogs, and princesses in
her illustrations. She currently lives in
northern Italy with her Prince Charming.

Uh-oh, Monster. You knocked over all those cans. You'd better clean them up! It's bad manners to run in a store.

Now you know to walk instead of run. But you'll need other good manners in the store, too. I'll show you.

A shopper is coming down the aisle. What do you do?

Watch where you're going, Monster! Don't bump into her. Move to the side and let her go by.

Good job, Monster. It's good manners to say you're sorry if you bump into someone. Now, how do you help Dad with the shopping?

Cookies, cookies, and more
cookies are not on the list.

Don't beg for foods that aren't on the list.
Instead, help find things that *are* on the list.

It's taco night, so taco shells are definitely on the list. Finding them for Dad is helpful.

Don't butt in front of that lady! Wait your turn.

Taco Shell
Taco Shell
Taco Shell
Taco Shell
Taco Shell
Taco Shell
Taco Shell
Taco Shell
Taco Shell

We also need salsa, but it's not in its usual place. How do you ask for help finding it?

Not quite, Monster. Try using polite words like excuse me, please, and thank you.

13

That was very polite, Monster. Look, there's
a girl in your class. What do you do?

Don't hide, Monster. When you see someone you know, say hello. Being friendly is polite, and it makes people feel good.

What do you do if Dad stops to talk to somebody?

Don't interrupt. Don't rush him. And don't wander off. Be patient. Dad is being friendly.

Sometimes the store has free samples of food. Only take one sample.

And be sure to say thank you! (But don't talk with your mouth full!)

It's time to check out. Help unload the cart.

Hey, no pushing! Roughhousing in
the store is definitely bad manners.

Good job carrying in groceries without being asked. I think you've learned your manners, Monst—hey you're not a monster. You're my brother Ben. Now, let's make some tacos!

GOOD MANNERS AT THE STORE

1. Walk, don't run in the store.

2. Watch for other people and move out of the way.

3. Help the grown-up you are with.

4. Don't beg for items not on the list.

5. Ask a store worker politely if you need help.

6. Say hello and be friendly to people you know.

7. Be patient if your parent stops to talk.

8. Take only one free sample.

9. No roughhousing in a store.

10. Help unload the cart and carry groceries.

READ MORE

Brainard, Beth. *Soup Should Be Seen, Not Heard! A Complete Manners Book for Kids.* Bingham, Mass.: Good Idea Kids, 2012.

Ingalls, Ann. *Good Manners in Public.* Mankato, Minn.: The Child's World, 2013.

Keller, Laurie. *Do Unto Otters: a Book About Manners.* New York: Macmillan, 2009.

Verdick, Elizabeth. *Don't Behave Like You Live in a Cave.* Minneapolis: Free Spirit Publishing, 2010.

WEBSITES

Can You Teach My Alligator Manners?
disneyjunior.com/can-you-teach-my-alligator-manners
Watch videos and do activities to learn about manners in all different places, including restaurants, school, and more.

Learn about Manners: Crafts and Activities for Kids
http://www.dltk-kids.com/crafts/miscellaneous/manners.htm
Try these songs, crafts, and coloring pages to learn and practice good manners.

Every effort has been made to ensure that these websites are appropriate for children. However, because of the nature of the Internet, it is impossible to guarantee that these sites will remain active indefinitely or that their contents will not be altered.